DATE DUE

EXTINCT BIRDS

and those in danger of extinction

Philip Steele

Franklin Watts
New York London Toronto Sydney

© 1991 Franklin Watts

First published in the United States
by Franklin Watts
387 Park Avenue South
New York, N.Y. 10016

Consultant: Professor Richard T.J. Moody,
BSc, Dip Ed, PhD, FGS
Design: Julian Holland Publishing Ltd
Picture Research: Jennifer Johnson
Illustrator: Mick Loates
Cartography: Gecko Ltd

Printed in the United Kingdom

Library of Congress Cataloging-in-Publication Data
Steele, Philip.
    Extinct birds/Philip Steele.
        p.   cm.
    Includes index
    Summary: Describes the physical
characteristics and habits of prehistoric
birds that are now extinct, such as
archaeopteryx, and those of species that
have either recently vanished or are
facing extinction.
    ISBN 0-531-11027-3
    1. Birds, Fossil – Juvenile literature.
2. Extinct animals – Juvenile literature.
[1. Birds, Fossil. 2. Extinct animals.]
I. Title.
QE871.S74   1991   90-41428
568-dc20   CIP   AC

Photograph acknowledgements
p5 Courtesy of the Natural History
Museum, London; p17 Sullivan & Rogers/
Bruce Coleman Ltd; P18 Gunter Ziesler/
Bruce Coleman Ltd; p19 Jeff Foott/Bruce
Coleman Ltd; p21 A.N.T./NHPA; p22
Eichhorn/Zigel/Frank Lane Picture
Agency; p23 Fritz Polking/Frank Lane
Picture Agency; p24 Jeff Foott/Bruce
Coleman Ltd; p25 John Shaw/NHPA; p27
Gordon Langsbury/Bruce Coleman Ltd.

Contents

As dead as a dodo

When we say that something is "as dead as a dodo," we mean that it has disappeared forever. It is strange to think that it is only since this bird became extinct that it has become famous.

The dodo was a large bird, about the size of a turkey. It was unable to fly and before the sixteenth century, it did not need to. It lived on the island of Mauritius in the Indian Ocean. There, it had no enemies. Then sailors from Portugal arrived. They were looking for fresh food to vary their diet on the long voyage between Portugal and the Far East.

The dodo was not used to being hunted and so was not afraid of its hunters. Its wings were small and weak, and it was unable to fly away.

Later, Dutch settlers brought dogs, cats, rats, pigs and monkeys with them. These too hunted the dodo or destroyed its nests and ate its eggs. In less than 200 years, the dodo became extinct.

▲ A major part of the dodo's diet was the fruit of the *Calvaria major*, or the dodo tree as it is now called. Scientists think that the action of the dodo's powerful gizzard crushed the seeds enough so they could germinate once they had passed through the dodo's body. Although the last 13 trees are still producing fruit and seeds, no new tree has appeared on Mauritius since the dodo became extinct. The dodo tree now faces extinction too.

DID YOU KNOW?
- The dodo was a giant relative of the dove.
- Since 1505, 24 kinds of birds have become extinct on Mauritius and on nearby islands.

Do & Given by C. Edwards F.R.S. A᷎ 175

1680 Dodo probably extinct.
1700 Réunion solitaire, a relative of the dodo, probably extinct.
1770 White dodo of Réunion extinct.
1780 Rodrigues solitaire extinct.

▲ The dodo was a plump bird. It had a massive beak and thick legs. Its feathers were downy, and plumes formed its tail.

The first bird

Birds have lived on our planet for about 150 million years. The first bird we know about is *Archaeopteryx*. Remains of six of these birds have been found, as well as a single feather. From these remains scientists can tell that *Archaeopteryx* had teeth, feathers and a long tail. There were claws on its wings that it probably used to help it to climb trees.

Scientists are not sure whether *Archaeopteryx* lived on open ground, or among the branches of trees. From the location of the remains, the scientists do know that *Archaeopteryx* lived near the coasts of warm prehistoric seas.

After *Archaeopteryx* became extinct, all kinds of birds evolved on earth. Some ate seeds or fruit. Others ate insects, fish or dead animals. Sometimes the climate changed. The plants and the animals that the bird ate changed as well. Birds that could not learn to adapt to these changes soon became extinct.

▶ *Archaeopteryx* was very like a reptile. Only two clues tell us that this was one of the first birds. It had feathers and it had a wishbone. The only animals with wishbones are birds.

DID YOU KNOW?
- *Archaeopteryx* was 35 cm (14 in) long, about the size of a crow.
- Remains of *Archaeopteryx* have been found in southern Germany.
- The hoatzin is a bird that lives in the forests of South America. Its young have claws on the front of their wings, just like *Archaeopteryx*.

---

150 million years ago: The first birds, such as *Archaeopteryx*, develop from reptiles.
1861 First *Archaeopteryx* fossil found.
1987 *Archaeopteryx* skeleton found in a limestone quarry.

Fossils

How do we know about prehistoric birds? After all, they have been extinct for millions of years. The answer lies in the rocks.

When prehistoric birds died, their bodies were often buried in mud or sand. The softer parts of the bodies soon decayed, but the harder parts like the bones remained. Over tens of millions of years the mud and the sand turned to stone because of the weight of new layers of mud and sand settling down on them and pressing water out. The remains of the bones left behind are called fossils.

Scientists study the rocks that enclose the fossils. By studying the fossils, they can work out how old the rocks are. They can also find out more about the birds and the world they lived in.

Ichthyornis

Remains of a seabird called *Ichthyornis* have been found in Kansas. From these remains, scientists think that it was like a gull in size and behavior and caught fish in its long jaws.

80 million years ago: *Ichthyornis* flies over the waves. *Hesperornis* feeds on fish.

TOOTHED BIRDS
- *Hesperornis* was a bird with short, stumpy wings. It could not fly, but swam and dived after fish which it caught in its long bill.

- *Ichthyornis* means "fishing bird."

▶ *Ichthyornis* was a primitive form of bird. However, scientists know that it could fly very well because of its strong wing bones.

Prehistoric hunters

After the death of the dinosaurs 65 million years ago, a group of large birds evolved which fed off small animals. One of them was *Diatryma*.

A flightless heavyweight

Remains of *Diatryma* have been found in Europe and in Wyoming. The bones show that it had small wings but because of its size it could not fly. It hunted small mammals and caught its prey by running after them.

A giant vulture

Only a few thousand years ago, a huge, soaring bird called *Teratornis* lived in California. *Teratornis* looked like a condor, had a wingspan of 4 m (13 ft) and weighed 20 kg (44 lb). *Teratornis* probably fed on dead animals.

▼ *Diatryma* was a giant bird about 2 m (6.5 ft) tall. It had a large head with a powerful, parrot-like beak. Its legs were stout and strong, and its clawed feet could destroy mammals such as early horses, which were about the size of a dog.

65 million years ago: Dinosaurs extinct.
55 million years ago: *Diatryma* roams the plains.
10 million to several thousand years ago: Giant vultures, like *Teratornis,* feed on mammals killed by wild animals.

▲ Remains of *Teratornis* have been found in California. The birds had fed on animals trapped in sticky tar pits at Rancho La Brea, and then become stuck themselves.

The moas

The moa family of birds developed over a period of 100 million years. Scientists think there may have been about 28 species altogether. Some had already become extinct by the time the Maoris arrived in New Zealand, but more were soon to follow.

For millions of years, the moas had no enemies. Then, about 1,100 years ago, the first Maori hunters arrived in New Zealand. They hunted the giant, wingless birds with spears. So many birds were killed that by 1500 only a few species were left. It was not until the middle of the nineteenth century, however, that the last of these giant, flightless birds was killed.

As well as hunting the moas, people also took their huge eggs. Records show that some of the eggs measured as much as 25 cm (10 in) in length. One of the largest eggs ever found was discovered in the grave of a Maori chieftain.

The Maori people used to have a saying which meant the same as "as dead as a dodo." It was "lost like a moa."

▶ The giant moa was 4 m (13 ft) tall and may have survived the longest of all the moas.

c850   Maoris arrive in New Zealand.

1500   Most species of moa hunted to extinction.

1640   Burly lesser moa extinct.

1670   Brawny greater moa extinct.

1800   Pygmy moa extinct.

1850   Giant moa extinct.

LOST BIRDS OF NEW ZEALAND
- The Stephen Island wren was discovered and died out in 1894. The last one was eaten by a lighthouse-keeper's cat.
- The huia, a wattled crow, had disappeared from North Island by 1907.
- The Auckland Island merganser, a kind of duck, was extinct by 1905.

The great auk

The stormy waters of the North Atlantic are home to many seabirds. There are lonely islands and high rocky cliffs where they can nest. It was in this type of habitat that the flightless great auk lived, swam and dived.

The decline of the great auk started very slowly in the tenth century. Sailors and fishermen occasionally hunted the great auk for food. By the 1500s, large numbers of the birds were being killed and their eggs taken. In the late 1700s the birds also started to be hunted for their feathers. The numbers of great auk were dropping alarmingly.

The last British great auk was clubbed to death on the remote Scottish island of Saint Kilda in 1840. The islanders said they thought it was a witch! Four years later, the last pair in the world were killed by Icelandic fishermen, who also smashed the very last egg.

▶ The great auk was an elegant, streamlined, diving bird which could not fly and was defenseless on land. It had a white breast, black back and a wedge-shaped beak.

DID YOU KNOW?
- The great auk was about 75 cm (2.5 ft) high.
- The great auk was once known as the penguin, but when European sailors reached the oceans in the southern part of the world, they used that name to describe the birds that they saw there.
- The great auk was also known as the garefowl.

1810 Great auk extinct in North America.

1844 Great auk extinct.

The passenger pigeon

Vast flocks of passenger pigeons, sometimes millions strong, once filled the skies of North America. They could fly long distances non-stop. However, in the space of about 50 years this marvelous bird became extinct.

In the 1850s there was a huge demand for pigeons in the shops. The adult birds were sold as a cheap meat dish, and the young birds were bought for a special meal as their meat was so tender. Even parts of the pigeons' insides were sold as medical cures. Their feathers were used to stuff pillows and quilts.

Passenger pigeons were also shot for "sport." People would release them from traps and then shoot at them. Thousands were massacred at their nesting sites.

By 1896 only 250,000 pigeons were left at one nesting site. The hunters found them and only 5000 birds survived. On 24 March 1900, the last passenger pigeon seen in the wild was shot by a young boy in Ohio.

▶ The passenger pigeon was a pretty dove, with a gray back and a pinkish breast. It lived in the woods and forests of North America where it fed on acorns, nuts, seeds, berries and insects.

DID YOU KNOW?
- Scientists estimate that the U.S. population of passenger pigeons may have numbered 9,000,000,000.
- The passenger pigeon could fly very fast and may have been able to reach a speed of 112 kph (70 mph).
- The last passenger pigeon of all died in Cincinnati Zoo in 1914.

1900 Last wild passenger pigeon shot.
1914 Last passenger pigeon dies in a zoo.

Under 100 still alive!

In prehistoric times, the climate and plant life changed gradually. Many animals, birds and insects were able to change and adapt gradually as well.

Today's high-speed changes mean that there is little time for creatures to adapt. The tropical forests are being cut down, swamps are being drained and hedging torn up. Hundreds of living things are now at risk. Some are on the verge of extinction.

The monkey-eating eagle

The Philippine monkey-eating eagle is listed as endangered. About 30 pairs survive, mostly in the forests of Mindanao.

Over the years, the monkey-eating eagle has been shot or captured for zoos. It is now protected by law, but its future remains uncertain. The forests it lives in are being cut down so that farms and towns can be built.

◄ The Philippine monkey-eating eagle is a magnificent bird of prey, measuring 95 cm (3 ft) in length. It uses its sharp talons and powerful, hooked beak to kill flying lemurs, squirrels, birds and monkeys. The tail is long and square-ended, and the wings are short but wide. This eagle has fierce, blue eyes, and a headdress of feathers forms a crest on its head. The bird has never been bred in captivity.

The California condor

The California condor is one of the rarest birds in the United States. Only 26 survive, and these are being held in captivity.

The number of condors has probably been in decline since prehistoric times. The bird can only produce one chick every two years. In the last 200 years, the places where the condor can live have become fewer and fewer. Farmers and hunters have shot it, disturbed its nests and poisoned its food. The future of the California condor depends on a breeding program.

▼ The California condor is 125 cm (4 ft) long, with black and white wings and a bald, orange head. In the wild, it finds its food by flying high in the sky, searching the ground for dead animals to eat.

The kakapo story

One of the rarest birds in the world today is the kakapo. It is a ground-dwelling parrot which lives on an island off New Zealand.

In the 1930s, kakapos survived only in the extreme south of New Zealand. Like other birds, they had been hunted and their nests destroyed. The birds were also often attacked by cats and rats. Scientists decided that the best way to save the kakapos was to take half of them north to Little Barrier Island.

Today only 14 female and 29 male kakapos survive. However, in March 1990 one of the young females, nicknamed "Heather," laid an egg. This was a special event because the females only lay eggs once in four years and no kakapo had been hatched for nine.

Unfortunately, although Heather's egg hatched, the chick died a few days later. Scientists are trying to find out more about kakapos so that they can save the birds from extinction.

▶ The kakapo has green, yellow and brown feathers. These help to camouflage it on the ground. The bird nests in holes and burrows.

DID YOU KNOW?
- The kakapo comes out at night to feed on berries, mosses and grasses, and nectar from flowers.
- The kakapo has a strong sweet smell like freesias.
- The wings of the kakapo are very weak and it can glide for only short distances.
- The kakapo is 60 cm (2 ft) in length.

1840 Kakapo extinct on Chatham Islands, New Zealand.

1927 Kakapo extinct on North Island, New Zealand.

1990 Kakapo egg laid on Little Barrier Island, New Zealand.

Guarding the nests

A lot of work is being done to save rare birds. This is necessary because some people try to steal rare eggs and sell them for high prices. Others steal the eggs of hawks and falcons and hatch them. The young birds are sold to falconers, who train them to hunt for sport.

In order to protect the eggs and young birds, the nesting sites of rare birds are guarded by bird-lovers day and night. In some places, hidden cameras are used.

In many parts of the world, rare birds are now protected by law. It has been made illegal to kill the birds, disturb their nests or to take the eggs. If anyone is found taking eggs, they can be fined large sums of money.

The red kite

The red kite was once very common in the British countryside. In the Middle Ages it even raided city garbage dumps. The red kite feeds on the carrion of small birds and mammals. This caused a problem for gamekeepers in the 1800s as the kite hunted among the birds that the keepers were trying to rear. As a result many birds of prey, including the red kite, were shot. By 1900, only a dozen red kites were left in the remote woodlands of Wales.

Bird-lovers protected the nesting sites, and today the number of the birds has increased to 140 in Wales, and 10 other birds have been reintroduced into England and Scotland. The threat remains, however. Ten red kite nests were robbed of their eggs in 1985. In 1989, 11 red kites were found dead; 8 of them had been poisoned.

▲ The red kite has long, narrow wings, a rust-colored body and a V-shaped, forked tail.

The osprey

The osprey is a graceful fish-hunter. It seizes its prey from the water with its talons. In North America and Asia it is still common. In Europe it has become very rare.

In 1916, ospreys bred for the last time at Loch an Eilean in Scotland's Spey valley. In 1955, however bird-lovers were amazed when a pair returned to Scotland to breed at Loch Garten. The site has been carefully guarded ever since, and about 20 pairs now nest in the Highland region.

▼ The osprey is a large hawk measuring 65 cm (2 ft) in length. Its sharp talons are covered with rough spikes which help it grasp its prey.

In need of protection

Bird protection does not end at the nesting site. Many birds migrate large distances each year, traveling over many countries. When small birds travel north after wintering in Africa, hundreds of thousands are shot and trapped by hunters as they cross the Mediterranean islands and southern Europe.

Many face other problems in the countryside, particularly the loss of feeding grounds. For instance, in the United States, drainage and coastal dredging, to make land suitable for agriculture, have destroyed acres of swamp and creek where birds used to feed. When bird numbers are very low, one very cold winter or a bad hurricane can be disastrous.

The whooping crane

In 1937, a National Wildlife Refuge was set up at Aransas on the Texas coast. This area of saltmarsh, grassland and woods is home to 350 kinds of bird. One of the most endangered is the whooping crane which visits the refuge between November and March.

In 1941, there were only 21 whooping cranes left. Then scientists started to track and observe the cranes, as well as raise them in captivity. Today there are 138 whooping cranes in the wild. There are also 16 birds in the Rocky Mountains which have been bred using sandhill cranes as foster parents. Another 46 birds are part of a captive flock in Maryland. Although the future of the whooping crane looks uncertain, scientists and bird-lovers are still working to protect the birds that winter at Aransas.

▲ The whooping crane is over 125 cm (50 in) tall. It is an elegant bird with a long neck and black, stiltlike legs. The plumage is snowy-white, but the bare face is red. The black-tipped wings span 210 cm (7 ft) and are powerful enough to carry the crane on its annual 3,000 km (1,800 mi) journey from Texas to its breeding grounds in north-western Canada.

The bald eagle

The magnificent bald eagle is the national symbol of the United States. It can still be seen soaring over the mountains and rivers of North America. However, its survival has been threatened.

The bald eagle's feeding grounds have been reduced. It is also being poisoned by pesticides.

Scientists have worked tirelessly to defend the bald eagle. For example, when many eagles were killed after building their nests on electricity pylons, special nesting platforms were built for them to use instead.

DID YOU KNOW?
- The female whooping crane lays only one egg.
- The whooping crane's cry can be heard 1.5 km (1 mi) away.
- The bald eagle returns to the same nesting site each year.
- The female bald eagle lays two eggs.

◄ The bald eagle belongs to the group of birds known as sea eagles, although it will often hunt inland along river banks and lake shores. It has a brown body with a white tail and head. Its powerful legs and sharp-clawed feet are designed for grasping slippery fish. Bald eagles also eat carrion, waterfowl and rabbits. The bald eagle's body length is 75 cm (30 in).

Around the world

All over the world, birds are threatened. The tropical forests are being cut down. This destroys the nesting sites of parrots and other tropical birds. At sea, oil spilled from tankers covers the feathers of seabirds with black, sticky tar that kills them. Millions of wild birds are sold to the pet trade every year. Cockatoos and macaws are especially at risk. One-fifth of all the bird species in the world are bought and sold by traders.

The World Wide Fund for Nature (WWF) has been fighting for animals and birds for many years. The International Union for the Conservation of Nature and Natural Resources (IUCN) is supported by 116 countries. Its scientists keep up-to-date records of birds and other creatures facing extinction.

In the past, zoos played a part in putting birds at risk. Collectors would take rare birds from their nests to supply the zoos. Today, some zoos and many bird reserves play an important part in saving threatened birds. They breed birds in captivity and then release them into the wild.

The néné

In 1949, the néné, or Hawaiian goose, was in danger of extinction. It was shot by humans and killed by dogs and mongooses. Three pairs were taken to the Wildfowl Trust at Slimbridge in England. Within 10 years, so many had been bred that it was possible to take some home to the Hawaiian Islands. Today, the néné is thriving.

▲ The International Council for Bird Preservation (ICBP) compiles up-to-date information on threatened birds. It publishes this information jointly with the International Union for the Conservation of Nature and Natural Resources (IUCN) as the *Bird Red Data Book*. The book gives the status of particular bird species as endangered, vulnerable or rare. This information helps scientists make crucial decisions on the conservation of our wildlife.

ICBP also conducts active conservation projects, ranging from forest management schemes to educational programs, all over the world.

▲ The néné has a
brown-gray body with a
white face. It is about
65 cm (2 ft) in length.

Glossary

bird A creature with two legs and two wings. Not all birds can fly. All birds have feathers and lay eggs. They have skeletons and are warm-blooded. This means that they can control their own body temperature.

climate The pattern of weather conditions experienced in a region over a long period. Changes in climate can affect a creature's chance of survival.

dinosaur One of an extinct group of reptiles which roamed the earth for 135 million years.

endangered At risk of dying out. Other terms used include "vulnerable" (at risk of becoming endangered), or "threatened."

extinct Disappeared, no longer living. Scientists now declare a creature to be officially extinct when it has not been seen in the wild for 50 years.

fossil The remains of an ancient animal or plant preserved in rock.

migration A journey made each season by birds or animals. Birds may migrate to find food supplies and to breed, or to escape from cold winters.

prehistoric Existing before people were able to write or keep records.

prey A living animal or bird which is eaten by another.

rare Being few in number. Rare birds are not necessarily in danger, but they obviously run a higher risk than more numerous birds.

reptile A scaly creature with a skeleton. Tortoises, snakes and lizards are all reptiles. The first birds developed from ancient reptiles.

talon The hooked claw of a bird of prey.

wishbone A forked bone supporting the breast of most birds.

Find out more

- Many big cities have a natural history or science museum, where you can see fossils of extinct creatures, and displays showing how they lived. The American Museum of Natural History in New York City is one of the best known of these museums.

- Are you interested in helping to protect endangered birds and animals around the world? The Wildlife Preservation Trust International sponsors the Dodo Club for young people. To find out more, write the Trust at 34th Street and Girard Avenue, Philadelphia, Pennsylvania 19104.

- The National Wildlife Federation answers queries about wildlife preservation, and publishes free and inexpensive materials on conservation. You can write them at 1412 16 Street, NW, Washington, DC 20036.

- The National Audubon Society, 950 Third Avenue, New York, NY 10022, seeks to protect birds and other wildlife and their habitats. The society conducts research programs to aid endangered species, such as the bald eagle and the whooping crane. Write to their Education Division to find out more.

- There are zoos in most regions of the United States. Do not go just to look – go to observe carefully how animals and birds live and behave. Find out if the zoo is working on any breeding projects.

- Stay at home! Build a bird-feeding station or simply put out food for the birds. Make a list of the species you observe.

Time chart

Years ago	Human history	Natural history
150 million		First birds evolve, such as *Archaeopteryx*.
90 million		True flying birds evolve.
80 million		*Ichthyornis, Hesperornis* alive.
65 million		Dinosaurs and flying lizards become extinct. Modern bird families begin to evolve.
55 million		*Diatryma* alive.
10 million		*Teratornis*, giant vultures evolve.
4 million	"Ape-people," such as *Australopithecus,* evolve.	
100,000	Modern people evolve, hunters with weapons of stone.	

HISTORIC PERIOD

12,000 B.C.		Climatic change and possibly hunting by humans lead to extinction of many large animals in the Americas.
10,000-1,500 B.C.	First farmers, in the Middle East. Domestication of farmyard birds, Asia.	Wild birds hunted and snared.
1,500 B.C.-A.D. 800	Classical period in Europe, followed by so-called Dark Ages. Clearance of forest, spread of human settlement.	Loss of habitat.
800-1450	Hunting, spread of farming, forest clearance. Europe begins to explore rest of world.	Loss of habitat.
1450-1700	Europeans colonize foreign lands, bringing firearms, introducing exotic animals.	Perhaps 5 bird species extinct, including dodo (1680).
1700-1800	European settlements spread in Americas. More efficient firearms for hunting. New farming methods, beginnings of industry.	Thirteen bird species extinct including Réunion solitaire (1700); white dodo (1770); Rodrigues solitaire (1780).
1800-1900	European settlements spread in Australia and New Zealand. Railways, large cities. Rapid firearms and hunting on a vast scale. Factories pollute air and poison rivers. Scientists learn about evolution and extinction.	Sixty-six bird species extinct including great auk (1844) and moas (giant moa 1850).
1900-	Motor transportation, factories, pollution, deforestation, pesticides. Growth of conservation movements, such as International Union for Conservation of Nature and Natural Resources, World Wide Fund for Nature, and International Council for Bird Protection. International treaties such as Convention on International Trade in Endangered Species	Possibly 55 bird species extinct so far, including passenger pigeon (1910). About 1,100 species listed as threatened by 1988. Widespread destruction of habitat and poisoning of prey.

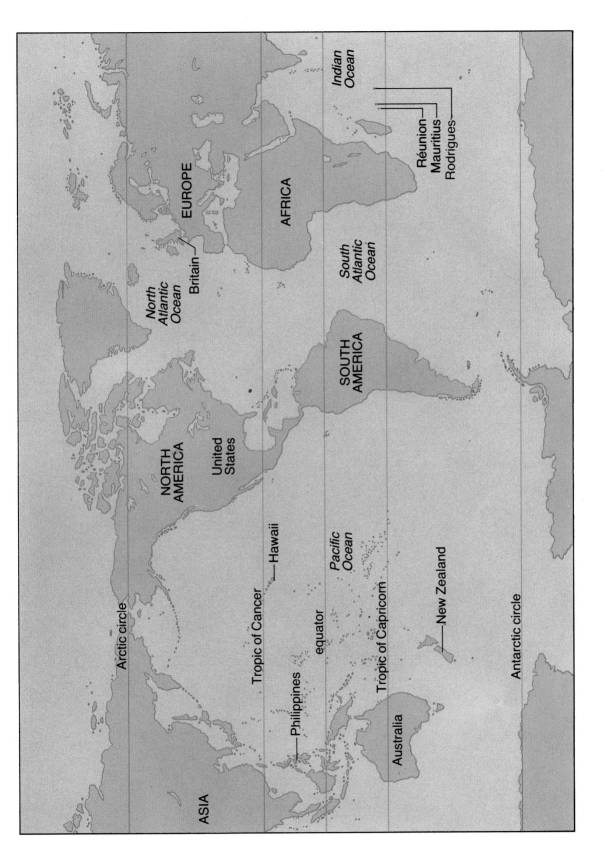

ASIA

NORTH
AMERICA

United
States

EUROPE

Britain

AFRICA

*North
Atlantic
Ocean*

SOUTH
AMERICA

*South
Atlantic
Ocean*

*Indian
Ocean*

Réunion
Mauritius
Rodrigues

Arctic circle

Tropic of Cancer

Hawaii

*Pacific
Ocean*

equator

Philippines

Tropic of Capricorn

New Zealand

Australia

Antarctic circle

31

Index